About
Skill Builders
Reading
Comprehension
Grade 3

W9-BRX-764

Welcome to the Skill Builders series. This series is designed to make learning both fun and rewarding.

This workbook offers a balanced mixture of humor, imagination, and instruction as students steadily improve their reading comprehension skills. The diverse assignments in this workbook are designed to enhance basic reading skills while giving students something fun to think about—from seeds to the Wright brothers.

Additionally, a critical thinking section includes exercises to help develop higher-order thinking skills.

Learning is more effective when approached with enthusiasm. That's why the Skill Builders series combines academically sound exercises with engaging graphics and exciting themes—to make reviewing basic skills at school or at home fun and effective, for both you and your budding scholars.

Credits:
Editor: Julie Kirsch
Layout Design: Mark Conrad
Illustrations: Janet Armbrust
Cover Concept: Nick Greenwood
www.summerbridgeactivities.com

Printed in the USA • All rights reserved.   ISBN: 978-1-60022-143-9

Table of Contents

Suggested Reading List

Adler, David
*Cam Jansen and
the Mystery of the
Television Dog*

Barrett, Judi
*Cloudy With a Chance
of Meatballs*

Berenstain, Stan and Jan
*Berenstain Bears Accept
No Substitutes
Big Chapter Books™*

Burton, Virginia Lee
Katy and the Big Snow

Catling, Patrick Skene
The Chocolate Touch

Cleary, Beverly
*Ramona Quimby,
Age 8*

Cole, Joanna
*The Magic School Bus
series*

Danziger, Paula
There's a Bat in Bunk Five

Donnelly, Judy
*A Wall of Names: The
Story of the Vietnam
Veterans Memorial;
Moonwalk: The First Trip
to the Moon*

Fox, Paula
Maurice's Room

**Gleiter, Jan and Kathleen
Thompson**
Paul Revere

Graff, Stewart
*Helen Keller:
Toward the Light*

Gutelle, Andrew
*Baseball's Best:
Five True Stories*

Havill, Juanita
Treasure Nap

Hidaka, Masako
*Girl from the Snow
Country*

Jeschke, Susan
Perfect the Pig

Jonas, Ann
Aardvarks, Disembark!

Jukes, Mavis
Blackberries in the Dark

Kellogg, Steven
Paul Bunyan; Chicken Little

Konigsburg, E. L.
The View from Saturday

Krensky, Stephen
*Witch Hunt: It Happened
in Salem Village*

Little, Emily
*Trojan Horse: How the
Greeks Won the War*

Lobel, Arnold
*Grasshopper on
the Road; Book of
Pigericks: Pig Limericks*

McMullan, Kate
Dinosaur Hunters

Osborne, Mary Pope
Moonhorse

Raskin, Ellen
*Nothing Ever Happens on
My Block*

Schroeder, Alan
*Minty: A Story of Young
Harriet Tubman*

Sharmat, Marjorie Weinman
Nate the Great series

Smith, Robert Kimmel
Chocolate Fever

Sobol, Donald J.
Encyclopedia Brown series

Steig, William
*The Amazing Bone;
Amos & Boris;
Sylvester and the
Magic Pebble*

Stock, Catherine
Emma's Dragon Hunt

Stoutenburg, Adrien
American Tall Tales

Waber, Bernard
Lyle, Lyle, Crocodile

White, E.B.
Charlotte's Web

Williams, Margery
The Velveteen Rabbit

Reading Comprehension • RB-904055

Trains go almost everywhere. There are almost 200,000 miles (315,000 km) of track in the United States. Maybe there is even a train track near your house. If there is, you need to learn a few rules so that you can stay safe.

Trains are big and heavy. If you are on the tracks, you are in danger. Even if an engineer sees you, it can take him more than a mile to stop the train.

Sometimes, people walk on or next to railroad tracks when they take shortcuts. They think they will know when a train is coming. They are wrong. They don't know. Trains run at all times, even at night.

When you have to cross a train track, be sure to go to a special crossing. Watch all of the signs. Never go around a gate that is down. Never cross the tracks when lights are flashing. Trains can be very fast and quiet. You may not hear one coming until it is too late.

Remember: Cross at special crossings. Pay attention to the signs. Don't ever play near train tracks. Stay safe!

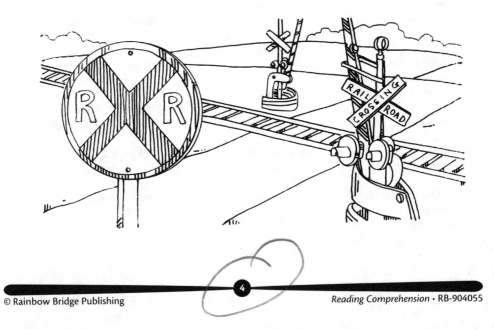

Reading Comprehension · RB-904055

Reading Comprehension

Read each sentence. If the sentence is true, circle **T**. If it is false, circle **F**.

1. One purpose of "Stay Safe" is to teach you how to ride a bike.　　　　T　　(F)

2. One purpose of "Stay Safe" is to give the history of trains.　　　　T　　F

3. One purpose of "Stay Safe" is to teach safety rules for railroad tracks.　　　　(T)　　F

4. One purpose of "Stay Safe" is to keep you from getting hurt by trains.　　　　(T)　　F

5. One purpose of "Stay Safe" is to sell train tickets.　　　　T　　(F)

6. One purpose of "Stay Safe" is to tell the exact times that trains run.　　　　T　　(F)

7. One purpose of "Stay Safe" is to make you laugh.　　　　T　　(F)

5

Costume Day

Rosa Ramos had wanted just one thing ever since her first year at Washington Street School. She wanted to win the Costume Day contest.

Costume Day was on a Saturday in April. Everyone came. There were game booths, balloons, and lots of good things to eat.

The best part of the day was the costume contest. A winner was chosen for every grade. There was also a grand prize. This year the prize was a free pass to the zoo.

Rosa thought about her costume all year. She looked at books and magazines to get ideas. She looked in shops and catalogs, too. Most of the kids wanted easy costumes. Rosa wanted hers to be special. She wanted a costume that was different from all of her friends' costumes.

One day, Rosa was doing a report on mammals for her science class. She saw a picture that gave her an idea for her perfect costume. She bought a striped tail and the ears with her birthday money. Then, she painted a white stripe on a black leotard. Next, she painted paws on an old pair of black shoes. Lastly, Rosa collected bottles of perfume from some of her neighbors and from her grandmother.

At last, the great day came.

Reading Comprehension

1. What animal costume did Rosa wear? <u>fox</u>

2. Read these two sentences about Rosa on Costume Day. Decide which sentence caused the other sentence to happen. Circle *cause* or *effect* below each sentence to show your answer.

   When Rosa got to the school playground, all of the other children screamed and ran away.

   cause   (effect)

   Rosa put on her costume and used all of the perfume.

   (cause)   effect

3. What does Rosa want? <u>adifrent costume then</u>
   <u>the others</u>

4. Do you think Rosa will win the costume contest? Why or why not?
   <u>the costume is cheartiv</u>

   _____

5. Number the following events in the order that they happened.

   <u>3</u>   Rosa puts on her costume.

   <u>1</u>   Rosa looks at books and magazines for good costume
        ideas.

   <u>2</u>   Rosa paints a white stripe on a black leotard.

Alisha Jones, Private Eye

Alisha hung a sign outside her clubhouse door. It read:

Alisha Jones, Private Eye

Her neighbor, Noah, rode down the driveway on his tricycle. He looked at the sign for a long time. Then, he looked around the yard. "Where is the yard sale?" he asked.

"There is no yard sale," Alisha told him. "The sign says I am a detective. I solve crimes, and I find things that are lost."

"If I lost something could you find it?" Noah asked.

"I could try," said Alisha.

Noah took Alisha to his house. They went into his room. Alisha looked around. She was not surprised that Noah had lost something. She was surprised that he ever found anything.

Noah went over to his closet. He took out a plastic car with a slot in the top. "This is my bank," he said. "Every week, I get 10 dimes for my allowance. I spend 5 of them at the mall. Then, I put the other 5 in here. On Monday, I had a lot of dimes. Now, they are all gone. Can you find them for me?"

"First, we need some clues," Alisha said. She shook the bank. She did not hear any dimes. Alisha opened the little door on the bottom of the bank. Two pieces of paper fell out. One was white, and one was green. When Alisha read what was written on the white paper, she tried not to laugh. The note said:

Dear Noah,

I needed some change for the wash. You had $4.50 in dimes. Here is $5.00. Thank you.

Love,

Mom

© Rainbow Bridge Publishing

Reading Comprehension

1. About how old is Noah? _____ ?

2. What clues do you have about Noah's age?

   _____ ?

   _____

3. On Alisha's street, what is the reason most people put up homemade signs? The signs say detective

   _____

4. Was Noah's room messy or neat? How do you know?

   it was neat

   _____

5. What was the green piece of paper in Noah's bank?

   his mom need mom money

6. Does Noah's mom have a washing machine in her house? How do you know? I know becase on the boten

   it say wash.

Brad's Robot

No one has seen Brad for hours. He has been in the basement building a robot. Brad's family is going to be surprised when they see the robot. Brad hopes they will not be mad. Brad used the trash can for the robot's body. He used a shoe box for the head. One of Mom's flowerpots made the perfect hat. He added a flyswatter to make one arm and a broom to make the other. Brad used some large nuts and bolts to make the robot's eyes and nose. Then, he painted a smile on the robot with his sister's nail polish. Brad thinks his robot is terrific! He hopes his family will think so, too.

Number the following events in the order that they happened.

___3___ Brad used a flowerpot for the hat.

___6___ Brad used nail polish for the smile.

___1___ Brad used a trash can for the body.

___5___ Brad used nuts and bolts to make the robot's eyes and nose.

___4___ Brad made one arm from a flyswatter.

___2___ Brad used a shoe box to make the robot's head.

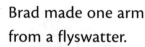

© Rainbow Bridge Publishing

Reading Comprehension • RB-904055

Be a Context Detective

Use the clues in the sentences to figure out the meaning of each word in **bold**. Circle the correct answer.

1. It was a **pleasant** day. The sky was blue and the sun was warm. We put on our swimming suits and ran down to the beach.

    A. dull   B. nice   C. sad

2. It was hot outside. Toby went to gather some eggs. All of the hens were asleep **beneath** the porch.

    A. under   B. above   C. on

3. Irma tripped and fell in the yard at lunch. She hurt her arm. The **ache** got worse when she carried a heavy box for Mrs. Wilson.

    A. dream   B. page   C. pain

4. Some dinosaurs were small, but brachiosaurs were **huge**.

    A. fast   B. big   C. old

5. We would not let a little rain **spoil** our trip to the zoo. We took our raincoats and umbrellas.

    A. ruin   B. fix   C. share

6. It was Clara's birthday. She was happy. She knew she would **receive** a gift from her best friend.

    A. give   B. chose   C. get

Seeds, Seeds, Seeds!

Many plants begin their lives as seeds. Flowers, garden vegetables, and trees all have seeds. If you have ever soaked a lima bean in water and then cut it in half, you have seen a baby plant inside of a seed.

Seeds come in many sizes. A coconut is a very big seed. Coconuts float on the ocean to new islands where they can grow into palm trees. Palm trees are big, but big plants don't always come from big seeds. A redwood, one of the biggest trees in the world, grows from a very tiny seed.

After seeds leave the plant, they need a good place to grow. A willow seed has to land in a good place soon. After a few days, the baby willow tree inside the seed dies. Most seeds last much longer than willow seeds. The seeds of a date palm grew after 2,000 years!

1. What does a coconut grow into? _Plam tree_

2. Do all big plants come from big seeds? _no_

3. What carries a coconut to a new island? _On the ocean_

4. Name one of the biggest trees in the world. _red woll_

5. How long did a date palm seed stay alive? _2,000 years_

© Rainbow Bridge Publishing

What's the Main Idea?

Read each paragraph. Then, decide which of the three sentences following the paragraph is the main idea. Write the letter of the correct answer on the blank.

___A___ 1. Laura has been watching her mom knit a sweater for weeks. When she asked her mother to make the sweater for her, she did not know how long it would take. Laura only knew she wanted a fluffy, blue sweater to wear skiing. As she watches, she almost feels sorry for asking for it. Laura thinks her mom must be really special to take so much time making something for her!

    A. A special mom knits a sweater.
    B. Laura learns her lesson.
    C. Laura learns to knit.

___A___ 2. Peter is a penguin with a problem. He is turning purple. In fact, he turns a bit more purple every day. Peter doesn't want to be purple. He is worried that his friends will laugh at him. His family will not talk to him. Peter will be embarrassed around other penguins. This really is a terrible problem.

    A. Being a purple penguin is a problem.
    B. Penguins search to find food.
    C. Turning purple is easy.

© Rainbow Bridge Publishing
Reading Comprehension · RB-904055

Title, Please (1-2)

Read each newspaper article. Choose the best title for each article from those listed on the newspapers below. Write the title on the line above the article.

1. _____

The place was Mudrock. It was 12:02 A.M. last Saturday night. Rangers in Sandstone Park found huge, mysterious footprints. Scientists looked at the prints, but no one knew what they were. They weren't like the prints of any dinosaur in town. The excitement grew with each day. Yesterday, Dino Dinosaur confessed. He made the prints with a bucket and a broom handle!

2. _____

Danny Dinosaur got a big surprise this week. Six weeks ago, Danny entered the Dinosaur Dream House Drawing. The drawing took place last Monday in Flatrock. Danny and his family were surprised and pleased to find they had won. "We just can't believe it!" Danny told reporters.

14

Title, Please (3-6)

3. _____

Debbie Dinosaur has written a book about dinosaur dancing. Her friends in Pebblebrook are very proud. The book is called *Dinosaur Dancing for Beginners*. The book is selling well. Miss Dinosaur is working on her second book. This one will be called *Cooking in a Cave*.

4. _____

The parents of Daisy Dinosaur are worried. Daisy has been missing all day. Police say she was last seen wearing a red hat. The police are not worried. They say that Daisy does this often. She can usually be found at her grandma's house!

5. _____

Everyone in Pebblebrook knows Della Dinosaur. For 12 weeks, Della has been collecting money. The money is for needy dinosaurs. Tuesday is the last day for the fund drive. If you can help, please call Della at 555-2121.

6. _____

The dinosaurs in Slateville will sleep easier tonight. The prowler has been caught. Police were stumped. For six weeks, residents had seen the shadow of the prowler near their windows and doors at night. Nothing was harmed, but folks were nervous. The prowler turned out to be little Andy Apatosaurus. Police found that Andy was walking in his sleep. Andy could not be reached for comment.

© Rainbow Bridge Publishing

A Class Trip to the Zoo

When Dylan's class went to the zoo, they found out that it was divided into sections. Each section represented a different kind of habitat. A *habitat* is a place where animals live.

The first section Dylan's class visited had animals from the mountains. In the Mountain Habitat, Dylan's class saw bears, golden eagles, deer, elk, bighorn sheep, and mountain goats. Dylan and his friends learned that not many animals lived high up in the mountains. Not many plants lived there, either.

The second section they visited had forest animals. In the Forest Habitat, Dylan's class saw raccoons, wolves, bobcats, wild boars, owls, and porcupines. Some mountain animals lived in the forest, too.

Next, they went to the Tropical Forest Habitat. They saw gorillas, chimpanzees, jaguars, toucans, parrots, and crocodiles. The chimpanzees were fun to watch. They were playing with their babies.

The last section of the zoo they visited had animals from the grasslands. Many of the grassland animals were from Africa. In the Grassland Habitat, Dylan's class saw giraffes, lions, elephants, zebras, hippopotamuses, and gnus.

© Rainbow Bridge Publishing

Reading Comprehension • RB-904055

Reading Comprehension

1. What does the word *habitat* mean?
   A. an apartment
   B. a place where animals live
   C. being late

2. In which section did Dylan's class see the giraffes?
   A. forest
   B. mountains
   C. grasslands

3. In which section did Dylan see the gorillas?
   A. grasslands
   B. tropical forest
   C. mountains

4. Which section had the porcupines?
   A. mountains
   B. forest
   C. grasslands

© Rainbow Bridge Publishing

Reading Comprehension • RB-904055

Ready for the Play-Off

Austin was too excited about the baseball play-off to think about the model volcano he and Ping were building for science class.

"Do you want to tear the paper into strips or dip them in paste and put them on?" Ping asked.

"Home run!" said Austin.

Ping looked puzzled. Austin's face burned with embarrassment. "I'm sorry. I was thinking about the game."

Ping laughed. "Oh!" he said. "Well, that explains it. Do you think we will win?"

"My big brother says Room 15 hasn't won a play-off in at least five years. Maybe we will be the first," Austin said.

Austin saw Mrs. Lee walking toward them. He picked up a piece of newspaper and tore it into strips. Ping understood. He dipped a strip into paste and smoothed it onto the side of the model volcano.

"You boys should start cleaning up now," Mrs. Lee said. "We don't want to be late for the game."

Austin and Ping looked at each other. They carried their model to the science table, put the lid on the paste container, bagged up the extra newspaper, and wiped down their work area. They were back in their seats and ready to go in five minutes. Some of the other groups took longer. "Home run!" Austin whispered to himself and smiled as he watched the clock.

© Rainbow Bridge Publishing

Reading Comprehension

1. Who is the main character in the story?
   A. Ping
   B. Austin
   C. Mrs. Lee

2. What does the main character want?
   A. to make a model volcano
   B. to win the play-off
   C. to clean up

3. Where does the story take place?
   A. on another planet
   B. in a classroom
   C. on the baseball field

4. When does the story take place?
   A. now
   B. a long time ago
   C. in the future

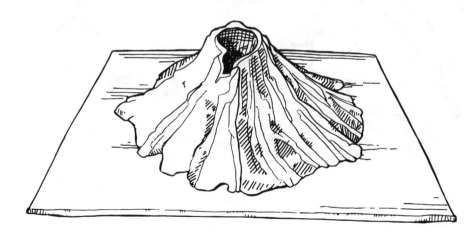

Reading Comprehension · RB-904055

Cockroaches

Cockroaches have been on Earth for millions of years. They were here before the dinosaurs. Cockroaches have hard shells that act like armor. They have good hearing and eyesight. A female cockroach gives birth to about 160 baby cockroaches every year. Cockroaches eat almost anything but can live nearly six weeks without food. They can even go 12 days without water. Cockroaches don't bite or hurt humans. So, why do people scream and run when they see them?

Reading Comprehension • RB-904055

Reading Comprehension

Read each sentence. Circle **F** if it is a fact. Circle **O** if it is an opinion.

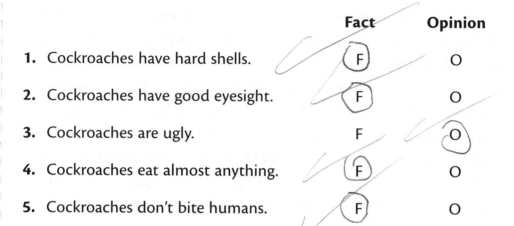

	Fact	Opinion
1. Cockroaches have hard shells.	F	O
2. Cockroaches have good eyesight.	F	O
3. Cockroaches are ugly.	F	O
4. Cockroaches eat almost anything.	F	O
5. Cockroaches don't bite humans.	F	O

Write one detail from the story in each oval to complete the story web. The main idea and one detail are done for you.

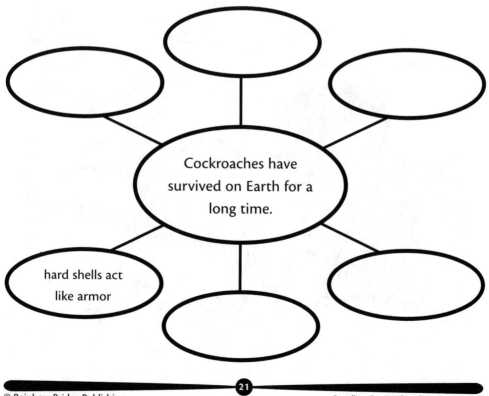

© Rainbow Bridge Publishing

Reading Comprehension • RB-904055

Ben's Leprechaun

Ben found a leprechaun in the park and was granted one wish. He thought about asking for everything he touched to turn to gold. Then, he remembered how that did not work out very well for King Midas. He thought about asking for all of the money in the world. Then, he remembered reading a story about that. It did not turn out too well, either. He thought about asking for a million dollars, but then he thought, "Is that enough? Who would I give money to? Who wouldn't I give money to? How will I know people like me for myself and not for my money?" After thinking carefully about the situation, he decided to settle for a hot fudge sundae. That would be the end of the story except that Ben dripped chocolate on his new shirt. The shirt was ruined, and his mother grounded him for a week.

Reading Comprehension • RB-904055

Reading Comprehension

Complete the story map.

Main Character

Setting

Plot (important events in the story)

You Need a Huggable Pet

Shouldn't everyone experience the joy of having a pet? You will love your Huggable Pet even more because you never have to feed or bathe it. It snuggles with you. It comes when you call. Your Huggable Pet even does tricks. Choose your favorite: Huggable Pets come in monkeys, dogs, cats, and birds. It's worth the joy at any price.

(Prices may vary. Some assembly required. Cost of clothes, pet toys, routine maintenance, and batteries not included.)

© Rainbow Bridge Publishing

Reading Comprehension

1. What is this advertisement trying to sell you?

_____

2. What does the advertisement say to convince you to buy this toy?
   A. It will make life easier.
   B. It will save you money.
   C. Everyone should have one.

3. What does the advertisement tell you is good about the toy?

_____

_____

_____

4. What does the advertisement tell you is bad about the toy?

_____

_____

5. What should you be careful about when buying this toy?

_____

_____

_____

© Rainbow Bridge Publishing

Reading Comprehension · RB-904055

The Wright Brothers

Orville and Wilbur Wright are famous American brothers. They owned a bicycle shop in Dayton, Ohio. Although they were interested in bicycles, they also loved the idea of flying. In 1899, they began to *experiment*, or try new ideas, with flight. They started by testing kites and then gliders, which are planes without motors. These tests taught them how an airplane should rise, turn, and come back to the ground. The brothers made over 1,000 glider flights at a field in Kitty Hawk, a village on the coast of North Carolina. This was fun but not good enough for them. Orville and Wilbur put a small engine on a plane they named *Flyer*. On December 17, 1903, Orville took the first motor-powered flight. It lasted 12 seconds. The brothers continued to experiment until they could stay in the air for over an hour.

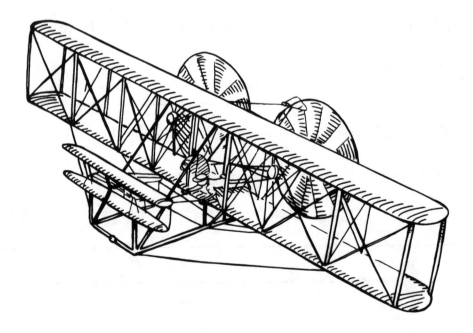

© Rainbow Bridge Publishing

Reading Comprehension • RB-904055

Reading Comprehension

1. What is the main idea of the story?

   A. Testing new ideas is not important.

   B. The *Flyer* was the first airplane.

   C. The Wright brothers were early pilots.

2. What does the word *experiment* mean?

   A. to try new ideas

   B. to test kites

   C. to stay in the air for one hour

3. Where did the brothers test their gliders and plane?

   Kitty hawk

4. How long did their first motor-powered flight last?

   it lasted 12 seconds

5. How did the brothers learn about what makes planes work?

   they put a small engine on a

   plane

© Rainbow Bridge Publishing

Photograph

Jack was not comfortable. His new shirt was too stiff and his tie felt tight. Mother had fussed over his hair, trying to get it to look just right. She made him scrub his hands three times to get the dirt from under his fingernails! Finally, his mom said he was ready. She smiled and said that Jack looked very handsome. Jack frowned, but he knew he could not tell his mom how he felt. This was important to her. Jack sat on a stool and looked at the camera. He didn't feel like smiling, but he did his best. "Perfect!" said the man behind the camera as he snapped the shot. Jack posed two more times. Then, the man said they were finished. The first thing Jack did was take off his tie!

© Rainbow Bridge Publishing

Reading Comprehension

1. What was Jack doing? Siting in a stool Smiling.

2. What clues tell you where Jack is? Going to take a Pic

3. How does Jack feel about this? He is not comfortable and he didnt feel like smiling.

4. What clues tell you how Jack feels? Behind the camera.

5. Who is the man that said "perfect"? _____

6. Why did Jack take off his tie? The tie was tight.

© Rainbow Bridge Publishing

Reading Comprehension · RB-904055

Mark Spitz

Mark Spitz is an American swimmer who set an Olympic record when he won seven gold medals at the 1972 Summer Olympic Games in Germany. Mark had been swimming in races since he was eight years old. By his late teens, he had already broken three world records in the freestyle and butterfly races. At the 1968 Olympic Games in Mexico, Mark hoped to win the gold medal, but he did not swim his best. He finished second in the butterfly and third in the freestyle. With heavy training, Mark Spitz came to the 1972 Olympic Games ready to swim his best. And, he did!

Reading Comprehension • RB-904055

Reading Comprehension

Use the story on page 30 to complete the crossword puzzle.

Across

2. How old was Mark when he began swimming in races?

3. Where were the Olympic Games held when Mark won seven gold medals?

5. Which stroke was Mark's best at the Olympics in Mexico?

7. Where were the Olympic Games held when Mark did not swim his best?

Down

1. How many world records did Mark set as a teenager?

4. What country did Mark represent?

6. How many gold medals did Mark win in 1972?

© Rainbow Bridge Publishing

Reading Comprehension · RB-904055

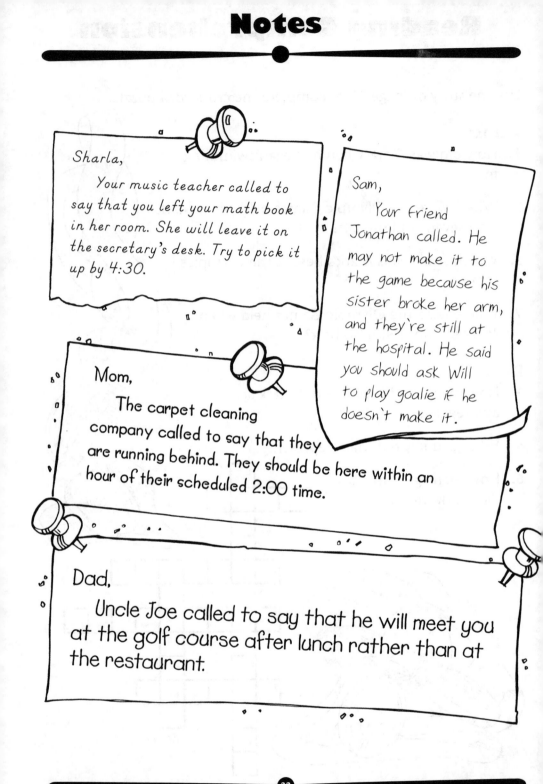

Sharla,

Your music teacher called to say that you left your math book in her room. She will leave it on the secretary's desk. Try to pick it up by 4:30.

Sam,

Your friend Jonathan called. He may not make it to the game because his sister broke her arm, and they're still at the hospital. He said you should ask Will to play goalie if he doesn't make it.

Mom,

The carpet cleaning company called to say that they are running behind. They should be here within an hour of their scheduled 2:00 time.

Dad,

Uncle Joe called to say that he will meet you at the golf course after lunch rather than at the restaurant.

Reading Comprehension

1. What book did Sharla leave behind at her music lesson?

   _____

2. Where will Uncle Joe meet Dad? _____

   _____

3. The carpet cleaners should be here by what time? _____

   _____

4. What position does Jonathan play? _____

   _____

5. Who broke an arm? _____

6. By what time should Sharla pick up her book? _____

7. Who should Sam ask to play goalie? _____

8. Will the carpet cleaners be early or late? _____

© Rainbow Bridge Publishing *Reading Comprehension* · RB-904055

Bats

Many people do not realize all of the things that bats do for us. Bats are special animals. They are the only flying mammals on Earth. Over 900 kinds of bats exist in the world today. The smallest bat is also the smallest mammal, about the size of a bumblebee. The largest bat has a wingspan of up to 6 feet (1.83 m). Bats help control the insect population. They use a sonar system to enjoy a nightly dinner of thousands of mosquitoes, mayflies, and moths. A bat makes a high-pitched sound that humans cannot hear. The sound echoes back and tells

the bat exactly where its next meal is. Although most bats just eat insects, some dine on fruit and the nectar of flowers. This is another way bats help humans. Bats pollinate and spread the seeds for many tropical trees. Mango, cashew, banana, and Brazil nut trees all depend on bats.

Reading Comprehension

1. What is the main idea of this paragraph? That bats control the insect population.

2. How many different kinds of bats are there in the world? Over 900 Kinds of bats.

3. What do bats like to eat? Insects, some dine on fruit.

4. How big is the largest species of bat? The largest bat has a wingspan.

5. What kinds of tropical trees depend on bats to spread their seeds for pollination?
   Mango, Cashew, banana, brazil nut trees

© Rainbow Bridge Publishing

Reading Comprehension • RB-904055

The Vanishing School Supplies

"Mom, I need more pencils for school tomorrow. I think I should get a lot," Raj said as he jumped in the car.

"Wow, you must really be working hard," replied Raj's mother. "You have used so many school supplies already. Last week, you needed scissors, and the week before that, it was glue."

The next morning, Raj put two packages of brand-new pencils in his backpack. When his mother picked him up after school, Raj said, "Hey Mom, can we swing by the store to get more colorful pencils?"

"What?" Raj's mother asked. "Raj, what is going on? You cannot possibly be using all of your supplies this quickly."

"Well, I am sharing them. It all started when Gerald made fun of Pete's binder. The cover was bent and dirty. It looked pretty bad. Then, Pete said that his family could not buy him a new one until his mom got paid again. I started thinking about it and realized that Pete never had his own scissors or glue. So, I gave him mine."

"Raj, I am very proud of you. I have an idea. Let's invite Pete to get ice cream with us after school tomorrow. I think you both deserve a little extra treat."

Reading Comprehension • RB-904055

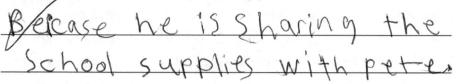

1. Why did Raj ask for so many new supplies?

   Because he is sharing the
   school supplies with peter.

2. Why didn't Pete have his own school supplies?

   His family coulb not buy him
   a new one until his mom got pe

3. Why did Gerald make fun of Pete's binder?

   Pete's binder was ~~cover~~ dirty
   and bent.

4. Why did Raj's mom feel proud of her son?

   Her son was sharing school
   supplies with pete.

The Littlest Bear

The littlest bear in Nunavut Park was also the loneliest bear in
Nunavut Park. He spent each day wishing for a friend his own size.
Then, one day he watched the older bears building snow friends.
Suddenly, the little bear knew how to solve his problem. He spent the
entire day building a snow bear to look just like himself. He wrapped
a scarf around his new friend's neck and slipped boots over his feet.
Then, the littlest bear realized that his friend could not play inside
the house. "That's okay," he thought. He ran inside, grabbed an old
blanket, and collected his toys. He spread the blanket out on the
snow and laid his toys on top. The littlest bear spent the whole winter
playing and laughing with his new friend. He never felt lonely for a
minute. Then one day, the summer air came to Nunavut Park, melting
the snow bear to the ground. At first, the littlest bear was sad, but as
he knelt down to the puddle, he saw his own reflection. He realized
that he had grown over the winter months and was no longer the
littlest bear. Even better, he was no longer the loneliest bear!

Reading Comprehension • RB-904055

Reading Comprehension

1. What was the littlest bear's first problem? The bear was alone.

2. How did he solve the problem? The littlest bear saw the older building snow friends.

3. What was another one of the littlest bear's problems?
The littiest bear saw his friend melting.

4. How did he solve it? he saw his own reflection he realized that he had grown over the winter mouts he was no longer the littest bear

Janek's Birthday Party

Janek is a third grader in Ms. Valdez's class. When Janek was five years old, his family moved from Warsaw, Poland, to Austin, Texas. Janek likes the warm weather, and he loves to swim. His birthday is in May. For his eighth birthday, he wants to throw a pool party. He and his mom made invitations for the party. Janek sent an invitation to everyone in his class.

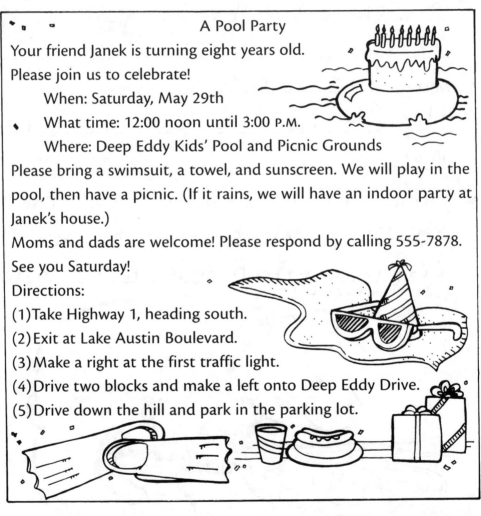

A Pool Party

Your friend Janek is turning eight years old.
Please join us to celebrate!

    When: Saturday, May 29th
    What time: 12:00 noon until 3:00 P.M.
    Where: Deep Eddy Kids' Pool and Picnic Grounds

Please bring a swimsuit, a towel, and sunscreen. We will play in the pool, then have a picnic. (If it rains, we will have an indoor party at Janek's house.)

Moms and dads are welcome! Please respond by calling 555-7878.

See you Saturday!

Directions:

(1) Take Highway 1, heading south.
(2) Exit at Lake Austin Boulevard.
(3) Make a right at the first traffic light.
(4) Drive two blocks and make a left onto Deep Eddy Drive.
(5) Drive down the hill and park in the parking lot.

Reading Comprehension

1. This selection is mostly about
   A. where to take swimming lessons.
   B. why you should wear sunscreen.
   C. how Janek invites kids to a party.
   D. Ms. Valdez's third-grade class.

2. Which of the following should people bring to Janek's party?
   A. sandwiches
   B. baseball hats
   C. balloons
   D. towels

3. If it rains, the party will
   A. be canceled.
   B. move to a place indoors.
   C. take place another day.
   D. continue at the picnic park.

4. According to the directions, what should you do after exiting at Lake Austin Boulevard?
   A. Take Highway 1, heading south.
   B. Take Highway 1, heading north.
   C. Make a right at the first traffic light.
   D. Make a left at the first traffic light.

5. The invitation asks people to
   A. call and say if they are coming.
   B. bring blankets for a picnic.
   C. prepare songs to sing for Janek.
   D. learn how to swim before the party.

© Rainbow Bridge Publishing

Marc Brown

Marc Brown is the best-selling author of the Arthur books. You may have read *Arthur's Birthday, D. W. Thinks Big,* or *Arthur and the True Francine.* These books and others tell about the life of an aardvark, his family, and his quirky animal friends.

Marc Brown enjoys drawing and telling stories. He had a grandma (Grandma Thora) who told wonderful stories. Mr. Brown got his love of telling stories from her. He told many stories to his own sons, who are now grown-ups. He especially liked to tell animal stories. One day, he told a story about an aardvark named Arthur. That was how the Arthur stories were born.

From the time he was six years old, Marc Brown has enjoyed drawing. Grandma Thora loved his drawings. She saved his drawings and told him to draw more. Now, Marc Brown draws the pictures and writes all of the stories for the Arthur books.

The first Arthur book was published in 1976. That book was called *Arthur's Nose.* In that book, Arthur had a long nose like a real aardvark. In the more recent books, Arthur's nose has gotten smaller. Mr. Brown shrank Arthur's nose so that he could show more expressions on Arthur's face. Since that first book, Marc Brown has written over 75 books about Arthur and his friends.

The ideas for the Arthur stories come from Mr. Brown's experiences when he was a child. He also gets ideas from his three children, Tolon, Tucker, and Eliza. In many of Marc Brown's books, you can find the names of his sons, Tolon and Tucker. He writes their names on packages in stores, on jackets, and in other small places. The next time you read an Arthur book, see if you can find their names!

© Rainbow Bridge Publishing

Reading Comprehension • RB-904055

Reading Comprehension

1. What does Marc Brown love to do?

   drawing, telling stories.

2. Where does Marc Brown get some of the ideas for the *Arthur* stories?
   A. from the zoo
   B. from watching television
   C. from his children
   D. from going on vacation

3. Where did Marc Brown get his love of storytelling?

   from GrandmaThora

4. If you could ask Marc Brown one question, what would you ask?

   _____

   _____

5. Imagine you are a writer and illustrator like Marc Brown. Draw your own storybook character in the space below. Then, on a separate piece of paper, write a story about your character.

Reading Comprehension · RB-904055

The Story of Clara Pickle

Everyone in town knew Clara Pickle. She was as dear and sweet as anyone could be. In fact, it was Clara Pickle's good nature that got her in trouble.

One day, a gray cat wandered into Clara's kitchen. Clara, who lived alone, decided to keep the cat as a pet. She was glad for the company. The next morning, she let the cat out for a breath of fresh air. When the cat came back that afternoon, he was no longer alone. He had brought his entire family and most of his friends with him. There were 34 cats in all!

Clara, sweet person that she was, adopted them all. In the next few days, the 34 cats had each added some friends. Clara Pickle then had 92 cats and kittens! She decided that 92 cats was too many, so she moved some of them to the barn. She gave a few dozen to her friends, too.

That first gray cat is still her favorite. Clara named him Dilly and gave him a nice bed on the floor next to her own.

Reading Comprehension

Number the following events in the order that they happened.

6   Clara had 92 cats and kittens.

8   Clara gave the gray cat a bed next to hers.

3   Clara took in the gray cat.

1   A lone gray cat wandered into Clara's kitchen.

4   The gray cat brought his family and friends back to Clara's house.

5   Clara gave some of the cats to her friends.

2   Clara let the gray cat out for some fresh air.

7   Clara moved some of the cats to the barn.

Horace Mann

In 1837, Horace Mann was a Massachusetts state senator. He voted to create the country's first state board of education. He was surprised and honored when he was chosen to lead the board. He took his new job very seriously. He traveled around the state and visited schools. He even went to Europe to find out how their schools were run.

Under Horace Mann's leadership, the Massachusetts Board of Education built a system of schools for all children. These schools were different in many ways. They had a school year of six months instead of just two or three. Teachers, who had not been trained before, attended special colleges. He also established district libraries.

Other states noticed the fine new schools in Massachusetts. They wanted good schools for their children, too. Soon, many states created school boards.

Reading Comprehension

Read the following sentences. If the sentence states an opinion, write an **O** in the blank. If it states a fact, write an **F**.

_f_ 1. A good school system is the most important part of a democracy.

_f_ 2. Horace Mann was a Massachusetts state senator.

_O_ 3. Europe still has better schools than America.

_f_ 4. Horace Mann headed the first state board of education in the United States.

_O_ 5. Under Horace Mann's leadership, the length of the school year doubled.

_f_ 6. Horace Mann went to Europe to see their schools and to talk with experts about education.

My Shadow

by Robert Louis Stevenson

1. I HAVE a little shadow that goes in and out with me,
2. And what can be the use of him is more than I can see.
3. He is very, very like me from the heels up to the head;
4. And I see him jump before me, when I jump into my bed.

5. The funniest thing about him is the way he likes to grow—
6. Not at all like proper children, which is always very slow;
7. For he sometimes shoots up taller like an India-rubber ball,
8. And he sometimes gets so little that there's none of him at all.

9. He hasn't got a notion of how children ought to play,
10. And can only make a fool of me in every sort of way.
11. He stays so close beside me, he's a coward you can see;
12. I'd think shame to stick to nursie as that shadow sticks to me!

13. One morning, very early, before the sun was up,
14. I rose and found the shining dew on every buttercup;
15. But my lazy little shadow, like an arrant* sleepy-head,
16. Had stayed at home behind me and was fast asleep in bed.

* that is, plainly such (a real sleepy-head)

Reading Comprehension

1. Which sentence best tells what the poem is about?

    A. A child goes to school and discovers his shadow.

    B. A child thinks about bird and animal shadows.

    C. A child describes his relationship with his shadow.

    D. A child and his shadow get lost on a playground.

2. Which word best describes how the speaker feels about his shadow?

    A. afraid

    B. amused

    C. bored

    D. quiet

3. The shadow is different from the speaker because it can

    A. get bigger and smaller.

    B. jump up and down.

    C. find dew on buttercups.

    D. play outside and inside.

4. What happens in the last stanza of the poem (lines 13-16)?

    A. The speaker goes to sleep.

    B. The speaker meets a new friend.

    C. The shadow stays at home.

    D. The shadow becomes larger.

5. Why did Stevenson write this poem?

    A. to explain how to make shadow animals on a wall

    B. to warn readers about losing their shadows

    C. to entertain readers with a familiar topic

    D. to inform readers about the types of shadows

© Rainbow Bridge Publishing

The Human Body

Table of Contents

© Rainbow Bridge Publishing

Reading Comprehension • RB-904055

Reading Comprehension

Read each question. Use the table of contents to decide in what chapter and on what page number you should begin to look for the answer to each question. Write the numbers on the blanks.

	Chapter	Page
1. How long does it take a bite of pizza to reach your stomach?	_____	_____
2. How does your body know when something tastes sour?	_____	_____
3. How many bones are in your skeleton?	_____	_____
4. What color is your blood?	_____	_____
5. How can you make yourself stronger?	_____	_____
6. How fast do nerve impulses travel?	_____	_____
7. Why do you have a belly button?	_____	_____
8. Are there more bones in your hand or your foot?	_____	_____
9. About how far can humans see?	_____	_____
10. How much of your body is made of water?	_____	_____

Campfire Walking Salad

Before you pick up your hot dog at the campfire, make a walking salad. You won't need a fork or plate for this salad. Just wrap the salad fixings in a piece of lettuce and carry it in one hand.

Ingredients:
large lettuce leaves
mayonnaise or peanut butter
salted Spanish peanuts
raisins
miniature marshmallows
raw carrot shavings

Directions:
Wash and pat dry several leaves of Bibb or leaf lettuce. Set out the ingredients on a table. Choose a lettuce leaf and spread mayonnaise or peanut butter on it. Then, add other toppings. Roll up the lettuce like a tortilla and eat.

Reading Comprehension · RB-904055

Reading Comprehension

Use the recipe to draw the steps for making a walking salad. Explain the steps and label the ingredients.

1.

2.

3.

4.

Helen Keller

Helen Keller was a well-known woman. She was born in 1880. When she was 19 months old, she suffered a terrible illness that left her unable to speak, hear, or see. For several years after that, young Helen lived in complete darkness and silence. She was angry and afraid and acted wildly.

When Helen was seven years old, her teacher, Ann Sullivan, taught her to "hear" and "speak" with her hands. After that, Helen learned quickly. She even learned to use her voice. Helen went on to college and graduated with honors.

Helen was very smart and dedicated. She wrote books and gave many speeches. She worked hard to teach others about coping with disabilities. She also worked against unfairness and violence against people. Helen Keller became very famous and lived to be 88 years old.

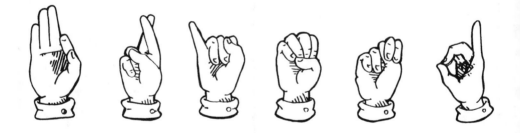

© Rainbow Bridge Publishing

Reading Comprehension • RB-904055

Reading Comprehension

1. List four of Helen Keller's greatest accomplishments (hard things she did).

    _____

    _____

    _____

    _____

2. Choose one of Helen's accomplishments. Write why you think it was harder for her to do than for a hearing, sighted person.

    _____

    _____

3. Write four words that describe Helen Keller.

    _____   _____

    _____   _____

4. Imagine you could not see, hear, or talk. What would be different about your day? Tell about one change that you would have to make in the morning, the afternoon, and the evening.

    Morning: _____

    Afternoon: _____

    Evening: _____

Reading Comprehension · RB-904055

Peterson's Pockets

I love pockets! When I pick out a new coat each year, I look for the coat with the most pockets. I especially like hidden pockets. I once had a coat with 12 pockets! I loved that coat.

I also love pants with lots of pockets. I love those pants that have pockets on the side of each leg. I like to put things in my pockets. I put money, bottle caps, cool stones, my yo-yo, notes from my friends, and other stuff I find in my pockets.

My mom doesn't like that I put stuff in my pockets. Sometimes I forget to take papers out of my pockets before my mom washes my pants. She says it makes an awful mess in the washing machine.

My dad said that long ago, pants didn't have any pockets! Back then, people wore little pouches that hung from their belts. I would have had to wear a pretty big pouch. My mom says that I would have to carry around a suitcase if I didn't have all of these pockets.

The first pockets on pants were little pouches sewn on the outside of pants. About 200 years ago, pockets finally were sewn on the inside of pants like they are now.

Someday, I'm going to invent a new place to hide a pocket. Maybe in 200 years, people will be talking about me and my supercool pocket. They will wonder how people ever got along without the "Peterson pocket."

Reading Comprehension • RB-904055

Reading Comprehension

This story was written from the point of view of Peterson, a boy who loves pockets. Write the same story from the point of view of either his mother or his father.

_____

_____

_____

_____

_____

_____

_____

_____

_____

_____

_____

_____

_____

_____

Colorado Attractions

Pike's Peak is the name of a mountain located in the Rocky Mountains of Colorado in the United States. It is not the highest peak in the state, but it is well-known for its amazing view at the top. When visiting, you can climb the mountain on foot or by horseback, cog railway, or car. Pike's Peak was named after the American explorer who discovered it in 1806.

The Royal Gorge is a deep canyon that was created by the rain and snow that run off the Rocky Mountains and into rivers. The Arkansas River runs through the bottom of the canyon, which is about 1,000 feet (305 m) deep. Visitors can enjoy an awesome view from the suspension bridge, which crosses the canyon.

© Rainbow Bridge Publishing

Reading Comprehension

Write the topic sentence of each paragraph from the article you just read. Then, write two details from each paragraph that support the topic sentence.

Paragraph 1

Topic Sentence: _____

_____

Supporting Detail: _____

_____

Supporting Detail: _____

_____

Paragraph 2

Topic Sentence: _____

_____

Supporting Detail: _____

_____

Supporting Detail: _____

_____

Reading Comprehension • RB-904055

Now or Then?

Have you ever been in a convertible car? If you had lived long ago when Henry Ford started making cars, you may have owned a convertible. Ford built the first cars that were low enough in price that many people were able to afford them. The cars could not go as fast as the cars we drive today, but they looked like a lot of fun!

Ford's cars were a little different from our modern cars. The cars did use gas, but the gas tank was under the driver's seat. A person had to lift the seat out to put gas in the car! Sometimes a car would not start in cold weather unless people poured hot water under the hood. Many of the cars did not have bumpers or mirrors because they cost extra money. Still, they were a great way to get around, just as our cars are today.

© Rainbow Bridge Publishing

Reading Comprehension • RB-904055

Reading Comprehension

Would you rather have a car from the past or a car from today? Make a list of similarities and differences to help you decide.

1. How cars of the past and cars of today are alike:

_____

_____

_____

_____

_____

2. How cars of the past and cars of today are different:

_____

_____

_____

_____

_____

James Cook

In 1768, James Cook sailed a long way for a strange reason. Scientists had discovered a way to see how far the sun was from Earth. But to help them do this, Cook would have to travel from England to an island in the South Pacific Ocean. Then, he and his crew would measure the time it took the planet Venus to move across the sun.

There were 94 people, including 11 scientists, on Cook's ship, the *Endeavor*. Their voyage was long, but Cook did everything he could to keep his men healthy. He made the men keep themselves and their beds clean. He brought fruits and vegetables with them to prevent the crew from getting scurvy, a disease caused by a lack of vitamin C. Cook also kept a goat onboard to give the men milk.

After eight months at sea, the *Endeavor* reached the island of Tahiti. There, they found friendly natives who had tattoos on their bodies. This was the first time the *Endeavor's* crew had seen this form of body art.

The crew *observed* Venus as they were told. Then, it was time to go. Cook had a new mission for them. They were to see if they could find a continent the size of Asia in the southern hemisphere. For many years, mapmakers believed that such a place existed. Cook was unable to find this continent. Instead, he found New Zealand and the eastern coast of Australia.

When Cook returned home, he was famous for the things he had discovered. James Cook was a different kind of explorer. Instead of seeking lands to conquer, he looked for new things to learn about and discover.

Reading Comprehension • RB-904055

Reading Comprehension

1. Choose a good title for this story.
    A. The Path of Venus   B. Conquering Tahiti
    C. The Lost Continent   D. Exploring for Science

2. How long did it take the *Endeavor* to reach Tahiti?

_____

3. What was Cook unable to find in the southern hemisphere?

_____

4. What did Cook have on board the ship to keep his crew from getting scurvy?

_____

5. What did the Tahitians have that the *Endeavor's* crew had never seen before? _____

6. Number the following events in the order that they happened.

_____ Cook became famous for the things he had discovered.

_____ The *Endeavor* started searching for a new continent.

_____ Cook left England for the South Pacific.

_____ The *Endeavor* reached Tahiti.

_____ The *Endeavor* reached Australia.

7. What does the word *observed* mean?
    A. watched   B. wrote about
    C. hid their eyes   D. drew pictures of

© Rainbow Bridge Publishing   *Reading Comprehension • RB-904055*

An Unusual Disease

Vance "Bo" Salisbury was sick because of a rare disease called flesh-eating bacteria. Very few people get this disease. Many don't survive it.

While playing soccer one day, Bo was kicked in the ankle. The injury didn't bother him until the next day. Then, the pain got so bad, his wife took him to the hospital.

The doctors couldn't figure out what was wrong with him, so they sent him home. The next day, he was sick to his stomach and unable to walk. His doctor sent him to the hospital again and started running tests.

The next morning, Bo was worse. He needed help breathing. Finally, the doctors were able to tell what was wrong. Bo had flesh-eating bacteria. They would have to put him on a strong medicine. The infected skin would have to be removed down to the muscle. As the disease spread, the doctors took off more skin. They didn't think Bo would live. Suddenly, the disease stopped spreading. The doctors said that it was a miracle.

To make sure all of the bacteria was gone, doctors removed much of the skin on Bo's leg. Healthy skin was taken from the rest of his body and put on the open wounds.

Today, Bo's leg isn't pretty, but, not only can he walk, he runs two or three miles a day. He's back at work and glad to be a survivor.

© Rainbow Bridge Publishing

Reading Comprehension

1. Choose another title for the story.

    A. Life in a Hospital
            B. Soccer Injuries

    C. Flesh-eating Bacteria
       D. Going Home

2. Why did the doctors keep removing Bo's skin?

_____

_____

3. What did the doctors use to cover the open wounds?

_____

_____

4. Number the following events in the order that they happened.

_____ Bo went back to work.

_____ Bo went to the hospital but was sent home.

_____ Bo was kicked while playing soccer.

_____ Skin was removed from much of Bo's leg.

_____ The doctors started running tests.

5. What can you tell about flesh-eating bacteria after reading about Bo's experience?

    A. Only men can get the disease.

    B. It's difficult for doctors to diagnose the disease.

    C. It's best to wait before going to the hospital if you think you have it.

    D. You can only get the disease if you play soccer.

A Camping Trip

Thomas and his parents went on a camping trip. They found the perfect spot beside a creek. Thomas and his dad set up the tent while his mom got out the supplies for dinner. When camp was set up, Thomas told his parents that he wanted to go exploring in the creek while the sun was still up. His father told him not to go too far from their campsite and to be careful.

Thomas rolled up his pant legs and waded into the water. He used a stick to poke a few leaves and rocks on the creek bed. Pretty soon he saw something that looked back at him. It was a snake. Thomas leapt out of the water and raced down the dirt path back to camp. Thomas jumped into the car and closed the door.

© Rainbow Bridge Publishing

Reading Comprehension

1. How did Thomas feel when he saw the snake? How do you know?

_____

_____

_____

2. Number the following events in the order that they happened.

_____ Thomas waded into the water.

_____ Thomas helped his dad set up the tent.

_____ Thomas jumped into the car and closed the door.

_____ Thomas saw a snake in the creek.

_____ Thomas told his parents he wanted to explore in
the creek.

3. What do you think Thomas did next? Finish the story.

_____

_____

_____

_____

_____

_____

Ruby Bridges

Have you ever not wanted to go to school? What if you knew that when you got to school, adults would yell at you to leave? What if you were only six years old when this happened?

That is exactly what happened to Ruby Bridges on Monday, November 14, 1960. That was the day the public schools in New Orleans were *integrated*. Ruby was the first African American child to go to an elementary school that was once only for white people.

Ruby's parents wanted her to go to a good school. The best school was just five blocks away from their home. However, it was only for white students. It took a new law, an order from a judge, and many police officers to see that Ruby could start going to that school.

The people in the city were not happy. They tried to get Ruby to stay home. People made threats on her family members' lives. Ruby's father was fired from his job.

On that first day, Ruby waited in an office all day. On her second day, she went to her classroom. She met her teacher, Mrs. Henry. The white parents had kept their children home. Ruby was Mrs. Henry's only student all year.

Ruby worked hard and got good grades. She grew up and went into business. She even helps out at her old school. Ruby is proud to have lived through those times. She knows that what she did helped all children today have a chance for a better education.

© Rainbow Bridge Publishing

Reading Comprehension • RB-904055

Reading Comprehension

1. Choose another title for this story.
   A. Equal Education for All
   B. Study Hard and You Will Do Well
   C. Good Schools Are Hard to Find
   D. Some People Can Be Mean

2. How far away did Ruby live from the school her parents wanted her to attend? _____

3. In what city did Ruby live? _____

4. What happened to Ruby's father when Ruby started at the new school? _____

5. Number the following events in the order that they happened.

   _____ A law was passed integrating public schools.

   _____ Ruby entered an all-white school.

   _____ Ruby waited in the principal's office on her first day of school.

   _____ Ruby went to business school.

   _____ Ruby met Mrs. Henry.

6. What does the word *integrated* mean?
   A. mixed
   B. decided
   C. separated
   D. helped

Francisco Vasquez de Coronado

Francisco Vasquez de Coronado was an important governor in New Spain (what is now Mexico), but he wanted more wealth. When he heard about the seven cities of gold, called Cibola, he had to go in search of this treasure.

Much of Mexico belonged to the Spanish in 1540. Most of the land to the north of Mexico had not been explored. Only a few Europeans had *ventured* into the American Southwest. Coronado became one of them.

With a group of 1,300 men, Coronado marched into what is now the state of Arizona. There, he met a tribe of Native Americans called the Zuni. They lived in Cibola, but Coronado didn't find any gold there. The people were very poor. Their homes were made of mud and straw.

Coronado told the Zuni that they had to become loyal to Spain. They didn't want to do this and decided to fight the Spanish. It was a large battle. The Zuni lost, but Coronado was almost killed in the fight.

Coronado still wanted gold. He sent out groups in different directions to see what they could find. One group found the Grand Canyon, but no gold. Another found more Native American villages, but still no gold. After two years of searching, Coronado did not find any gold.

When he returned home, Coronado was called a failure. He lost his job as governor and died 10 years later. Coronado never understood that he had done something more important than finding gold. His explorations had opened the American Southwest to the rest of the world.

Reading Comprehension

1. Which of the following best describes Coronado?
   A. friendly
   B. greedy
   C. happy
   D. angry

2. What was the name for the seven cities of gold?

   _____

3. What was Mexico called when Coronado was the governor?

   _____

4. Number the following events in the order that they happened.

   _____ Coronado heard about the seven cities of gold.

   _____ The Zuni fought a large battle with the Spanish.

   _____ Coronado entered what is now the state of Arizona.

   _____ Coronado was called a failure.

   _____ A group of Coronado's men discovered the Grand Canyon.

5. What does the word *ventured* mean?
   A. dared to go
   B. escaped
   C. settled
   D. read

6. Why do you think Coronado was called a failure when he returned home to Mexico?
   A. He didn't win the battle with the Zuni.
   B. He didn't discover the Grand Canyon himself.
   C. He didn't find any gold on his journey.
   D. He didn't conquer the seven cities of gold.

Critical Thinking Skills

What Does it Mean?

Read the following passages. Then, circle the choice that gives the best meaning for the saying in **bold** type.

1.   Sydney invited 12 friends to her birthday party. She wanted to know how many of her friends would be able to come, so at the bottom of each invitation she wrote **RSVP** and her phone number.

   A. Bring a present.
   B. Please reply.
   C. Please call if you are going to be late.

2.   Every week, Andrew's father gave him an allowance of $1.00. One week, Andrew's father got a bonus at work. That week, Andrew got $5.00 from his father.
      "Will I get five dollars every week from now on?" Andrew asked.
      "No," his father said. "Just **once in a blue moon**."

   A. once a month
   B. when the moon is blue
   C. every once in a while

3.   When Ethan's father lost his job, the whole family had to help out. Ethan's mother went back to work, and his sister got a babysitting job. Ethan helped, too. Instead of buying lunch in the cafeteria, he made himself a sandwich every day. It was how he helped his family **make ends meet**.

   A. have enough money
   B. find a job
   C. tie a rope

© Rainbow Bridge Publishing

Reading Comprehension • RB-904055

Critical Thinking Skills

What Does it Mean?

Read the following passages. Then, circle the choice that gives the best meaning for the saying in **bold** type.

1.   When Alexander moved, he made many new friends, but he didn't forget his old pals. One weekend, he invited John and Ryan, two friends from his old school, to come for a visit. He also invited Samuel and Noah, two of his new friends. At first, John and Ryan were very quiet. Alexander was confused. He thought they would all have fun together. Then, Alexander had an idea. He grabbed his baseball and his bat. They all went to the park. It really **broke the ice**.

   After they hit a few balls, all of the boys were talking and laughing as if they had known each other since first grade.

   A. warmed them up

   B. made them more at ease

   C. helped their game

2.   Abigail was having the worst day of her life. First, she got a D on her history report. Then, she fell down on the playground and tore her new jeans. Finally, her best friend announced that she was going to move to Ohio and they would probably never see each other again. Abigail put her head down on her desk. Her teacher patted her on the back. "**When it rains, it pours**," she said. "I've had days like that, too."

   A. When one thing goes wrong, many things go wrong.

   B. Things go wrong, then it rains.

   C. It always rains when friends move away.

© Rainbow Bridge Publishing   *Reading Comprehension* · RB-904055

Critical Thinking Skills

A Mixed-Up Story

Number the following sentences in the order they happened. Rewrite them in order on the lines below as a paragraph.

_____ Zach and his friends sat together on the bus.

_____ His mom dropped him off at the school.

_____ When Zach woke up, he was excited about the class picnic.

_____ He loaded his backpack into his mom's car and jumped in the front seat.

_____ The bus left the school on time. The trip had begun!

_____ His friends David and Anthony were waiting for him at the school.

_____ He packed some sunscreen, a hat, and a bag lunch into his backpack.

_____

_____

_____

_____

_____

_____

_____

Reading Comprehension • RB-904055

Critical Thinking Skills

Make a Word

How many new words can you make using the letters in the words below? The first one is started for you.

FLOWERPOT

top

owe

NOTEBOOK

FRIENDSHIP

Make it a contest! Have a friend write the same three words on a separate piece of paper. See who can come up with the most new words. Or, set a time limit to see who can think of more words faster.

Critical Thinking Skills

Homophone Word Search

Read the following words. Write the homophone for each word on the line. Then, find and circle your answers in the word puzzle below.

1. dear _____

2. hare _____

3. pail _____

4. sea _____

5. tow _____

6. flee _____

7. blew _____

8. feat _____

9. tale _____

10. plain _____

a	r	h	l	d	e	e	r
p	w	i	m	e	x	l	u
b	a	k	u	m	n	u	f
t	k	l	h	e	g	s	l
r	b	c	e	b	w	d	e
r	t	u	o	l	j	t	a
i	s	p	l	a	n	e	h
a	l	h	y	v	e	e	s
h	e	t	o	e	a	f	k

Reading Comprehension • RB-904055

Critical Thinking Skills

Using Context Clues

There is a nonsense word in each pair of sentences. Write a word on the line that makes sense in place of the nonsense word.

1. Green is my favorite *prackle*.

My cousin likes to *prackle* with markers and crayons.

The nonsense word *prackle* means _____ .

2. Olivia likes to *verg* her bicycle after school.

I think the best *verg* at the amusement park is the carousel.

The nonsense word *verg* means _____ .

3. Jamal likes to *jeffa* soccer at the park on the weekend.

My sister Alice was the lead in the school *jeffa* this year.

The nonsense word *jeffa* means _____ .

4. My friend and I *blape* a good movie last weekend.

Bo's dad used a small *blape* to trim the tree by their house.

The nonsense world *blape* means _____ .

© Rainbow Bridge Publishing

Reading Comprehension • RB-904055

Answer Key

Page 5, Stay Safe
1. F; 2. F; 3. T; 4. T; 5. F; 6. F; 7. F

Page 7, Costume Day
1. a skunk; 2. effect, cause; 3. She wants to win the Costume Day prize.; 4. Answers will vary.; 5. 3, 1, 2

Page 9, Alisha Jones, Private Eye
1. between 4 and 5; 2. He can ride a tricycle by himself, but he can't read.; 3. when they have a yard sale; 4. It is messy. Alisha is surprised he can ever find anything.; 5. a five-dollar bill; 6. No, she has to use the coin laundry.

Page 10, Brad's Robot
3, 6, 1, 5, 4, 2

Page 11, Be a Context Detective
1. B.; 2. A.; 3. C.; 4. B.; 5. A.; 6. C.

Page 12, Seeds, Seeds, Seeds!
1. a palm tree; 2. no; 3. the ocean; 4. redwood; 5. at least 2,000 years

Page 13, What's the Main Idea?
1. A.; 2. A.

Pages 14–15, Title, Please
1. Big Mystery Solved; 2. Dinosaur Wins Dream House; 3. Local Author Writes Book; 4. Dinosaur Missing; 5. Time Runs Out for Della's Drive; 6. Prowler Caught

Page 17, A Class Trip to the Zoo
1. B.; 2. C.; 3. B.; 4. B.

Page 19, Ready for the Play-Off
1. B.; 2. B.; 3. B.; 4. A.

Page 21, Cockroaches
1. F; 2. F; 3. O; 4. F; 5. F
Details can include: were here before dinosaurs; have good hearing; have good eyesight; can go 12 days without water; eat almost anything; can go nearly six weeks without food; give birth to about 160 babies a year

Page 23, Ben's Leprechaun
Main Character: Ben; Setting: the park; Plot: Ben found a leprechaun in the park. He thought about things to wish for. He wished for a hot fudge sundae. He dripped chocolate on his shirt. His mother grounded him for one week.

Page 25, You Need a Huggable Pet
1. a Huggable Pet; 2. C.; 3. It can do tricks, you don't have to feed or bathe it, it snuggles with you, and it comes in a variety of animals.; 4. nothing; 5. extra costs, some assembly required

Page 27, The Wright Brothers
1. C.; 2. A.; 3. Kitty Hawk, North Carolina; 4. about 12 seconds; 5. by experimenting with kites and gliders and then with engines

Page 29, Photograph
1. He is having his picture taken.; 2. sitting on the stool, looking at the camera; 3. He doesn't want to do it.; 4. His shirt was too stiff, his tie was too tight, and he frowned.; 5. the photographer; 6. It was not comfortable.

Answer Key

Page 31, Mark Spitz
Across: 2. eight; 3. Germany;
5. butterfly; 7. Mexico; Down: 1. three;
4. America; 6. seven

Page 33, Notes
1. math book; 2. at the golf course;
3. by 3:00; 4. goalie; 5. Jonathan's sister;
6. 4:30; 7. Will; 8. late

Page 35, Bats
1. Bats do many things for us.; 2. over
900 kinds; 3. Bats eat insects, fruit,
and the nectar of flowers.; 4. It has a
wingspan of 6 feet (1.83 m); 5. Bats
spread seeds for mango, cashew,
banana, and Brazil nut trees.

Page 37, The Vanishing School Supplies
1. He was giving them to Pete.; 2. His
family could not afford to buy supplies.;
3. Pete's binder was broken and dirty.; 4.
Raj had helped Pete by sharing supplies
with him.

Page 39, The Littlest Bear
Answers will vary. Possible answers
include: 1. He was lonely.; 2. He made
a snow friend.; 3. His new friend could
not play inside.; 4. He played outside.

Page 41, Janek's Birthday Party
1. C.; 2. D.; 3. B.; 4. C.; 5. A.

Page 43, Marc Brown
1. He loves to draw and write.; 2. C.;
3. from his Grandma Thora;
4-5. Answers will vary.

Page 45, The Story of Clara Pickle
5, 8, 2, 1, 4, 7, 3, 6

Page 47, Horace Mann
1. O; 2. F; 3. O; 4. F; 5. F; 6. F

Page 49, My Shadow
1. C.; 2. B.; 3. A.; 4. C.; 5. C.

Page 51, The Human Body
1. 4, 51; 2. 7, 90; 3. 1, 3; 4. 5, 64; 5. 2, 25;
6. 3, 39; 7. 6, 72; 8. 1, 3; 9. 7, 90; 10. 5, 64

Page 53, Campfire Walking Salad
Pictures will vary but should show the
steps in this order: 1. Wash the lettuce.;
2. Spread mayonnaise or peanut butter
on the lettuce.; 3. Add other toppings.;
4. Roll up the lettuce like a tortilla and
eat it.

Page 55, Helen Keller
1. Answers will vary. Possible answers
include: learned to speak with her
hands, learned to speak with her voice,
went to college, wrote books, taught
others, worked against unfairness.; 2.
Answers will vary. Example: It was hard
for Helen to learn to use her voice
because she couldn't hear herself.; 3.
Answers will vary.; 4. Answers will vary.

Page 57, Peterson's Pockets
Stories will vary.

Page 59, Colorado Attractions
TS—Pike's Peak is the name given
to one of the mountains located in
the Rocky Mountains of Colorado.;
Supporting details will vary.
TS—The Royal Gorge is a deep canyon
that was created by the snow and rain
that run off the Rocky Mountains and
into rivers.; Supporting details will vary.

Answer Key

Page 61, Now or Then?

Answers will vary. Possible answers include: Alike: They both use gas. They are a great way to get around. They are both available as convertibles. Different: Old cars could not go very fast. In old cars, the gas tank was under the front seat. Some old cars did not have bumpers or mirrors.

Page 63, James Cook

1. D.; 2. eight months; 3. a continent the size of Asia; 4. fruits and vegetables; 5. tattoos; 6. 5, 3, 1, 2, 4; 7. A.

Page 65, An Unusual Disease

1. C.; 2. to make sure all of the bacteria was gone; 3. healthy skin from other parts of his body; 4. 5, 2, 1, 4, 3; 5. B.

Page 67, A Camping Trip

1. Thomas felt afraid. He leapt out of the water, ran down the path, and jumped into his family's car.; 2. 3, 1, 5, 4, 2; 3. Answers will vary.

Page 69, Ruby Bridges

1. A.; 2. five blocks; 3. New Orleans; 4. He was fired.; 5. 1, 2, 3, 5, 4; 6. A.

Page 71, Francisco Vasquez de Coronado

1. B.; 2. Cibola; 3. New Spain; 4. 1, 3, 2, 5, 4; 5. A.; 6. C.

Page 72, What Does It Mean?

1. B.; 2. C.; 3. A.

Page 73, What Does It Mean?

1. B.; 2. A.

Page 74, A Mixed-Up Story

6, 4, 1, 3, 7, 5, 2

Page 75, Make a Word

Answers will vary but may include: Flowerpot: flow, plow, prow, row, tow, low, ow, owe, owl, few, pew, to, too, two, flower, lower, power, tower, towel, pot, plot, rot, lot, flop, top, lop, fool, pool, tool, foot, root, troop, loop; Notebook: note, not, ton, to, too, ten, book, took, nook, boot, bone, tone, bet, net; Friendship: friend(s), end(s), send, fend(s), rend(s), fried, shied, den(s), pen(s), hen(s), pie(s), die(s), ship, hip(s), dip(s), drip(s), rip(s), ripe, nip(s), din, dine(s), dish, fin(s), fine, fish, pin(s), pine(s), shred, shin, shine, hid, hide(s), rid, ride(s).

Page 76, Homophone Word Search

1. deer; 2. hair; 3. pale; 4. see; 5. toe; 6. flea; 7. blue; 8. feet; 9. tail; 10. plane

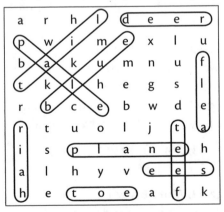

Page 77, Using Context Clues

1. color; 2. ride; 3. play; 4. saw

Reading Comprehension · RB-904055